Piano • Vocal • Guitar

Love Songs of the '90s

W9-CQA-629

This publication is not for sale in the E.C. and/or Australia or New Zealand.

ISBN 0-7935-4593-5

HAL•LEONARD™
CORPORATION

7777 W. Bluemound Rd. P.O. Box 13819 Milwaukee, WI 53213

ALL FOR LOVE

from Walt Disney Pictures' THE THREE MUSKETEERS

Words and Music by BRYAN ADAMS,
ROBERT JOHN "MUTT" LANGE and MICHAEL KAMEN

ANYTIME YOU NEED A FRIEND

Words and Music by MARIAH CAREY
and WALTER AFANASIEFF

If you're lone-ly and need a friend___
When the sha-dows are clos-ing in ___

and trou-bles seem___ like they nev-er end,____
and your spir-it dim-in-ish-ing,____

just re-mem-ber to keep the faith _____
just re-mem-ber you're not a-lone _____

BEAUTIFUL IN MY EYES

Words and Music by
JOSHUA KADISON

BEAUTY AND THE BEAST

from Walt Disney's BEAUTY AND THE BEAST

Lyrics by HOWARD ASHMAN
Music by ALAN MENKEN

Female: Tale as old as ___ time, *Male:* song as old as ___ rhyme. *Both:* Beau-ty and the ___

Beast.

Beau-ty and the Beast. ___

Can You Feel The Love Tonight

from Walt Disney Pictures' THE LION KING

Music by ELTON JOHN
Lyrics by TIM RICE

THE COLOUR OF MY LOVE
from the Musical SCREAM

Words and Music by DAVID FOSTER
and ARTHUR JANOV

EVERY HEARTBEAT

Words and Music by AMY GRANT,
WAYNE KIRKPATRICK and CHARLIE PEACOCK

Lyrics:
Hear me speak what's on my mind.
Clas - sic case of boy meets girl.
Let me give this tes - ti - mon - y.
Mov - ing in the same di - rec - tion.
Re - af - firm that you will find _____
You're not ask - ing for the world, _____

EMOTIONS

Lyrics by MARIAH CAREY
Music by MARIAH CAREY, DAVID COLE and ROBERT CLIVILLES

Moderate Dance tempo
no chord

mf

Fmaj7 Em7 Am

Fmaj7 Em7 Am

Fmaj7 Em7 Am

You've got me feel-ing e-mo - tions _____

Fmaj7 Em7 Am

deep-er than I've ev - er dreamed_ of. _____ Woh, ____ oh. _____

When you're look-ing in - to _____ my _____ eyes _____ you make me feel so _____ high!

(Vocal 1st time only)

(1st time only)

FOREVER IN LOVE

By KENNY G

(D.S. - Sax solo ad lib.)

(Sax solo ad lib.)

Repeat and Fade

FIELDS OF GOLD

Words and Music by
STING

GOOD FOR ME

Words and Music by JAY GRUSKA, AMY GRANT,
TOM SNOW and WAYNE KIRKPATRICK

MCA music publishing

HOPELESSLY

Words and Music by RICK ASTLEY
and ROB FISHER

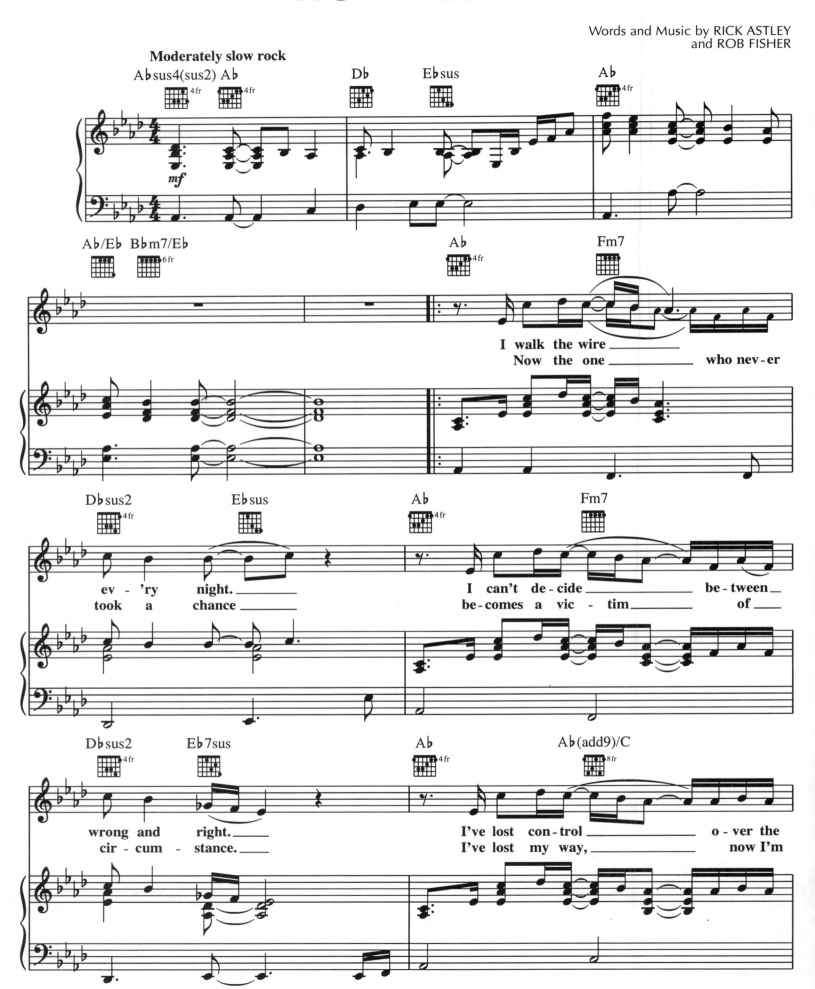

58

HOW AM I SUPPOSED TO LIVE WITHOUT YOU

Words and Music by MICHAEL BOLTON
and DOUG JAMES

HAVE I TOLD YOU LATELY

Words and Music by
VAN MORRISON

I'D DO ANYTHING FOR LOVE
(BUT I WON'T DO THAT)

Words and Music by
JIM STEINMAN

76

I WONDER WHY

Words and Music by GLEN BALLARD
and CURTIS STIGERS

Love _____ is a hun - ger _____ that
I'm no _____ an - gel _____ with

I'LL MAKE LOVE TO YOU

Words and Music by
BABYFACE

Close your eyes, make a wish, and blow
lax, let's go slow. I ain't

IN THE STILL OF THE NITE
(I'LL REMEMBER)

Words and Music by
FRED PARRIS

IF I EVER FALL IN LOVE

Words and Music by
CARL MARTIN

IF I EVER LOSE MY FAITH IN YOU

Words and Music by
STING

LOVE TAKES TIME

Words and Music by MARIAH CAREY
and BEN MARGULIES

let you _ go. _ I can't es-cape the pain. _ in - side _ 'cause love _ takes _ time. _

I don't want to be here. I don't want to be _ here _ a-lone. _

Oo. _

You might say_ that it's o-ver. _ You might say _ that you don't_

THE POWER OF LOVE

Words by MARY SUSAN APPLEGATE and JENNIFER RUSH
Music by CANDY DEROUGE and GUNTHER MENDE

The whis-pers __ in the morn - ing __

of lov-ers sleep - ing tight

are roll - ing by __ like thun - der now,

SAVE THE BEST FOR LAST

Words and Music by PHIL GALDSTON,
JON LIND and WENDY WALDMAN

Just when I thought _____ our chance_ had passed, _

you go and save ____ the best ___ for last. _

All of the nights_ ___

SOMEONE LIKE YOU
from JEKYLL & HYDE

Lyrics by LESLIE BRICUSSE
Music by FRANK WILDHORN

THE SWEETEST DAYS

Words and Music by JON LIND,
PHIL GALDSTON and WENDY WALDMAN

SOMETIMES LOVE JUST AIN'T ENOUGH

Words and Music by GLEN BURTNIK
and PATTY SMYTH

But there's a dan-ger in lov - ing some-bod - y too much, and it's

sad when you know ___ it's your heart ___ {you / (D.S.) they} can't trust. ___ There's a

rea - son why peo - ple don't stay ___ {where / who} they are. ___ Ba - by,

some-times love just ain't _ e - nough. _

THAT'S WHAT LOVE IS FOR

Words and Music by MARK MUELLER,
MICHAEL OMARTIAN and AMY GRANT

VISION OF LOVE

Words and Music by MARIAH CAREY
and BEN MARGULIES

Lyrics:
I had a vi-sion of love ___ and it was all that you've giv-en to me. ___ I had a vi-sion of love ___ and it was all ___ that you turned out __ to be, ___

A WHOLE NEW WORLD
(ALADDIN'S THEME)
from Walt Disney's ALADDIN

Music by ALAN MENKEN
Lyrics by TIM RICE

154

YOU MEAN THE WORLD TO ME

Words and Music by BABYFACE,
L.A. REID and DARYL SIMMONS